Poetic Superhero

Poetry Blog: www.amazulugaming.com
Instagram: Onepoeticgamer
Twitch: www.twitch.tv/onepoeticgamer

© 2020 Billy Williams, Jr. All rights reserved, including the right to reproduce this book or portions thereof in any form whatsoever. Contact AmaZulu Gaming, LLC for info at the following e-mail: onepoeticgamer@amazulugaming.com

ISBN 978-0-578-22934-8

Published by
AmaZulu Gaming, LLC

All art work done by
Christopher James Rowland

contact info for CJ Rowland
Instagram: istimyouleye

Final Edition
Printed in the United States of America

Table of Contents

Who Is This Guy

A Poet, Out of Order……………………………….9
Feel This…………………………………………...11
Freestyle Friday -Part VI-……………………….13
I Am Who I Be For a Reason……………………..16
It's Hip-Hop (Version 2)………………………….17
It's The Afro Baby………………………………..18
Soul Beacon……………………………………….22

Poetic Superhero

Cool Burn…………………………………………24
Depressurize………………………………………24
Don't Take It Personal…………………………...25
Freestyle Friday -Part IX-……………………….28
Inside The Eye of a Hurricane…………………...30
Let Me Tell You………………………………......32
Relax, Relax……………………………………….34
Rock-Solid-Words……………………………...…36
Soul Brother Number II………………………….39
This is To You Pops……………………………….40
Truth……………………………………………….42
What-Is-Stress…………………………………….45
What's Behind a Bullet…………………………..51
When I Realized I………………………………..54
You Ain't Got No Power…………………………54

There is No Tomorrow

A Reason..56
Displaced...56
At Thirty..57
Elimination...58
Freestyle Friday -Part X-........................61
Here's To My Education.........................63
Hunger..65
In That Number......................................68
One More Time......................................74
Proving My Innocence............................75
She Endured the Long Nights.................77
Soul Trap...79
Third World Vision.................................81
This Thing Called Poetry........................85
To You, The Victim (Revised)................89
Trapped Inside My SELF.......................93
What American Dream...........................94
What Are You Saying.............................98
When She Realized 98
Whoever You Are, I Accept....................99

Acknowledgments
(Original acknowledgments made in 2005 with a few updates)

Much thanks to Christopher James Rowland for the art work and the positivity you've always shown me. A true friend is hard to find and a good brother is rare in these days and time, so I am glad to say you are both a brother and a friend to me. You are the big brother I stay looking up to and I hope I can accomplish the high poetic goals you said I can.

Much love to Mom, Dad, Big Sis, Shanga, Pat, Kobee, Anim-Addo, "Pretty Boy" Mark, Gary and Uncle R. To my boys in Worthdale, it's always love here and I haven't forgotten you all. To my boys I directed in Herm Hall, I hope you guys are doing your thing. San Lamb, there's no way I would leave you out of the acknowledgments. Wanted to ask you one thing though..."who's my DJ?"

To all the elementary school kids I worked with that never stop acting crazy...I hope you are still crazy, I liked you that way. To all the high school and middle school kids I work with, we taking over! Grandma (R.I.P.) and Aunt B, thanks for the listening ear and wisdom you've given. To anyone who's given me encouragement, thanks.

My Big Brother Chuck, man, where would I be if the Universe never set us up to rock whatever place we work in. Thank you for taking on the big brother role without me even asking. One love big bro.

I would be remiss if I didn't send a LOUD shout out to my poetic sister Ebony. You're so special, you get a paragraph to yourself. I know we had our ups and downs but that's what soul siblings do. May God bless you and your artistic work.

I want to put this paragraph in for the financial supporters that helped fund AmaZulu Gaming, LLC. A list of names is not important because it is a community that is helping to keep this all moving.

One love to my brother Ra. Without you pushing and prodding me to bring my older poetry to light, there may not have been a rebirth of Poetic Superhero so soon. Thanks brother.

This has been a long time coming. Honestly, it's right on time for me. Peace.

Preface

This poetry book was written for the many people looking for a superhero. When was the last time you picked up a comic book and saw someone like me saving the day? Times are changing and there are others out there that are like me. Please note that one of my super powers is poetry. If you choose to read this book, I may be able to bring a different energy/vibe to you. I won't limit what type of energy/vibe this could be because it's your imagination I want to spark, as well as, your heart, mind and spirit. So, know that this book is dedicated to all those looking for a superhero. I'm glad you have picked up this poetry book, now let me save your day.

Who is this Guy?

A Poet, Out of Order

I'm a poet, out of order
lost in my notes
gotta get ready with no practice
I might choke
I'm a poet, out of order
I missed church last week
and I skipped devotion
I'm a poet, out of order
thinking sick thoughts
like sexin', cab confessions
since I missed church last week
I gotta learn my lesson
I'm a poooet, out of orrrder
words don't make sense
was on the mic but couldn't rock it
was on life support but got pulled from the socket
I'm a poet, out of order
in-between, kinda, sorta
maybe I outta, get focused
cut off the TV, turn down the music
would you believe me
that I'm a poet, out of order
no son, no daughter
got a million poems worth a quarter
yes I'm a poet, out of order
out of order, out of order
damn now I'm skippin'
as if punched by De La Hoya
out of order, I'm a poet

dyslexic flow, but you wouldn't know it
a poet, out of order
slamming words, on the verge, I will be heard
cause I'm a poet, out of order
running out of breath
am I the last one left
that's a poet, out of order
out of order, out of order.

Feel This…

Feel this pure essence
this vibe that is the equivalent
of taking speed on top of caffeine
never mind I'm doped up on morphine
wait, here's what I mean
I'm that grass that's green on both sides
be it on the sideline or up in the frontline
I'm past my prime
yet I'm prime time
see me trade in sunshine for shade
just to be on the cool side of things
I seek days of constant storm
just to see if you can stand the rain
no pleasure without pain
but what do I stand to gain
for fame that never pays
consider me, washed up enough to be
considered for the come back
even though I lead the pack back on track
cause it's like that
state facts like opinions
so we can debate the truth of the matter
in sections
split the pie up in eight different ways
and drive them different directions
I'm stressin'
just so minds can be fed
bringing some life to the dead

often thought I'm mislead
cause I keep numbers red
-just to stay hungry-
this way, my success can continually repeat
like the thrill you get from first time kisses
or
second hand disses
that come through internet mixes
and these
hardcore wanna-bes
that beat up keys when responding to
poetry I wrote last week
that honestly, was weak
but kicked the cheeks
of those that thought they wanted beef
as I, serve flows that go hard in the paint
but be easy like Sunday morning
half the things I hear today
has the kid yawning
but since I've been to long with this
let's finish with the same amount of dopeness
used and abused just to create this need for a period
of convalescence

Feel – This – Pure – Essence.

Freestyle Friday -Part VI-

I've sat up for days
watched light turn into darkness
as my pencil lead faded
writing different poetic styles
went the extra mile
and when my well went dry
I used tears and sweat to fuel my midnight oil
someone said I had to rock this
so I went and got Jesus
then called Puffy
so we can Make the Band
and as my fingertips turned raw
from constant scribin'
I grabbed a prosthetic hand
to make up the difference
the over under got me as the next best thing
Vegas got me 7 to 1
but skip them,
you should always bet on black
and B-Dot just got out from under the sun
so while I may not be "the one"
I am one to be the sacrificial poet
so I'm in demand at poetry slams
even though I've never made the team
you need me
like periods monthly
cause when I cycle, I've done more than hit singles
I'm doubling up for triple the action
then I'm running home

been doing this back since Lindsay Lohan
was Trapping Parents and looking geeky
now we both in rehab
it's just I'm in poet's anonymous
and I can't seem to put my pen down
cause when I do
I end up in a freestyle
and all the while they treating me like a star
but I'm super
so while I might not be what you're use to
I'm definitely up there in the top 10%
of the poets who came to wreck ish
you want to get high
hit spliffs
not your thing
sniff this
next line of words cause I'm serving them heavy
and when the levee broke
it was me with the saints running it back
you want flow
I got that
but if you looking for hustle
I suggest you move to the right
I was born at midnight
but not last night
and they not locking me down
for selling dope on the block
I'm national now
that's why we spittin' on different plots
yet we in your spot
and if you looking for something hot
then (whoosh) you got B-Dot

and whether you knew it or not
it's going down right here
keep ya focus right here
and if you wit it
let me here you say yee-aaaaaaaahhhhh!!!!!

I Am Who I Be For A Reason

I probably destroy half my chances
by cursing, being loud
and taking nonessential stances
speaking my mind leaves promotion behind
because I sometimes do things
at inappropriate times
not afraid of anyone standing or that's sitting down
so I'm taken as a threat
won't take mess from no clown
and as a result of public actions
they say I'm a bad influence
but I am who I be
don't let this finger change your appearance
I'm like nobody else, why you getting embarrassed
here comes my outburst, I really don't care if
you can't take it because
this is usually how I'm heard
and I'm not concerned if you feel I'm absurd
because I'll always do what others say I can't
and society won't dictate my actions
be I seen as chump or champ
I am who I be
not changing for nobody
especially if you think
I should be like somebody…else.

It's Hip-Hop (Version 2)

Hip-Hop, I get so influential when I
Beat Box, my lyrics are so serious I
De-Tox, I really have no money so it's
Fort Knox, I'm wishing I was living as the
Sure Shot, but I'm not
so I gots, to do what I gots to do it's
too hot, my feet move as I groove but
I'm not, so what's up with the props that
you pop, on dead lock, I'm so shock I
for-got,
to bring you back on to rock
to bring you back on to stomp
to bring you back on to knock
completely out the box,
cause it's uhhh
Hip-Hop, I get so influential when I
Beat Box, my lyrics are so serious I
De-Tox, my payload is depleted so I
restock, the lyrics they like bullets so now
you're shot, can feel it in your spirit cause it's
Hip-Hop, I'm always wearing Nike never
Reboks, a secret you can't keep it cause I'm
unlocked, forever in your memory I am
now notched, I whisper
got you wonderin' what uhhh,
I got, will end this on the rhythm we call
Hip-Hoooooooooopppppppppp.

It's The Afro Baby
(read to "T" Plays it Cool by Marvin Gaye)

I'm a '70's afro child baby
my soul carries the burdens
as well as the good times
in pant size pockets,
we call memories
I call it history
so don't act like you don't know who I be
when I ask
-remember me?-
Yeah, if you keep staring
I'll suggest you take a picture
won't be a need for an autograph
my good looks are just as good as cash
cause,
I-am-the-one…
I stop waiting for you to tell it
and started believing
watched out for the devil since he be deceivin'
when I feel like it,
I can get so fresh and so clean, clean, clean…
even in some sweat pants
I make it happen cause you can't
the revolution is here, the revolution is here…
the revolution is…me,
the revolution is,
this poetry…
it's the afro baby
'70's extraordinary B.E.

Billy Eugene, nicknamed Be Easy
and that's a fact jack
I raise my right fist and represent
black power
-no-
soul power
so fly I make time fall back a hour
so at night I'll have more time to shine
because the sunlight be stealing mine
but I'm not jealous
no need to be over zealous
I got that ambition baby
so don't come with no but's, if's or maybe's
that's shady
and I'll have you know I'm the truth
so stop searching
why work harder and not smarter
got your body hurting
mind twerking, heart lurking
didn't I tell you I was the one
one of God's sons that discovered long ago
his purpose,
it's-the-afro-baby
coming to you live and direct
here on the set
if I put this in a book then I guess
you'll be receiving this second hand
but for those on hand
you're dealing with a man
who means what he says
and says what he means

so please, please listen
because when I'm quiet
I'm observing, I'm learning
how to get rich
and not die tryin'
how to keep climbin'
my way to the top
and I thought I told you
I won't stop
it's too hot below
and the further I go towards the light
the more this feels right
I don't even need a mic
get close to me,
I can make this intimate
get real serious,
finish most sentences with exclamation marks
but the question remains
if it's a B and a Dot
what comes after the period?
Some say the kid isn't good
cause his words are only spoken
when he reads,
but please believe I'm not affected by that
in fact, at least I can read
and write,
so when I ghost the lines others say on the mic
who's the real poet?
On another note
I hope you're enjoying yourself
cause I am

on this, poetic epic
let's move to the next lesson
since they say I'm the professor
a teacher,
that's willing to give but only if you reach
you got to want this
you have to have it,
"it" being the information
what you do with it is power
Knowledge is Power
only if you use it
cause when you abuse it
you'll end up like mad scientist
I hope you get
-the point-
cause it's the afro baby
'70's baby, saying stuff you should already know
and if I made you hot
then cool out,
I'll let the music flow
cause this could go on and on
but then I'd be the show
so I'll pause right here for now
and somebody else, can go.

Soul Beacon

I'm sending love vibrations
spiritually,
so those in tune
listening
know my position
coordinate to my location
or know that when I appear
where they are
love is near,
making sure I can hear
on the same frequency
be that source of healing
tingling, in ways available
when systems are open
encircling that thing
that brings smiles to lips
warmth to hearts
sparks to central nervous systems
resulting in a feeling we box up
as love,
but rises above
the human experience
in coexistence
with the energy
sent spiritually
as love vibrations
from my soul beacon.

Poetic Superhero

Cool Burn

My passion is locked into me
like the "force"
deep within this energy bubbles
like hot springs
called on at will
by my will
my passion is untapped
all that needs to be done
is focus,
using senses to make sense of the world
the emotion
the intangible feeling
felt at the tips of fingers
with each contraction of my heart
breathe in, breathe out
this soul power
this…unabridged…
passion.

Depressurize

Pain is a venom my memory taste
and my pencil does a poor job
cause my lead doesn't erase
but I escape through context
written rebellious at times
to get the evil thoughts up and out of my mind.

Don't Take It Personal

Since minds don't go on vacation
tell'em I'm waitin'
cause I'm debatin'
on how to get people conversatin'
on my past and present situations
there's no faking
I don't even care if they are hatin'
as long as I'm their concentration
there'd be no segregation
because I desegregated the anticipation
by relating my soul to this poetic revelation
and, I know I got some of these cats shaking
cause they thinkin' they might be forsaken
it's just the first go round
but my conversation
will be repeated 3 times so there's no mistaken
you'll hear everything I'm sayin', I'm praying
cause if this was black jack
you can take the hit because I'm stayin'
causing some thoughts to be in desiccation
that means, I'm causing dehydration
and desolation with desecration
which serves as by-products of procrastination
so make haste in retaliation
or disassociate from the cypher association
because disarrangement is next to Satan
like cleanliness is on God's list
of things religious freaks think will save them from
hells gate and

since minds don't go on vacation
remember I said I'm waitin'
I'll take on the whole nation
because nobody knows who they're facin'!

Freestyle Friday -Part IX-

3...2...1...
the horn blows and the game is over
and they should've kept me in the draft
but now you let loose a beast
that's got poetry in pockets
in his draws
coming out the back of his ass
since he can't get it out his mouth
so potent
I touched the caged bird and made it speak
words - spoken
I'm tote'n bullets
just to use the lead to etch-a-sketch my verse
it's ten times worse when I'm hype
you'd think I got struck by lightning
cause I'm lighten up mics
lighten up spaces with thoughts so serious
my words reached off the page
smacked this kid
now he's furious
and you may feel like I'm delirious
so go ahead, put me away in Bellvue
and really, that's cool
cause the next time I come back
I'll have seven mad poets bringing hell too
so what'cha gon' do
when you see the white's of his eyes
cause by this time
I've shot 9 times within 9 lines

in the confines of young minds
and when the police come
they'll find black on black rhyme was the crime
if you not poetically inclined
then take a piece of my mind
cause the fact that I shine like the sun
means you need to get shades
cause I got words for days
and I'm not paid enough to do it
but screw it
we can take this world wide
and add different dialects to it
because the same result will be brought to this
point, that will be made
we can do this backwards
and from Black we shall unfade,
out the shade and into this craze
of freestylin'
if you thought I was wildin'
wait till I get started
it'll be like I farted and you can't escape the room
driving you up the wall
driving you crazy
I'm driving Miss Daisy
you can't phase me
even if you tased me
back in '92 they use to page me
now they use satellites to locate me
and since it's pay day
which makes it Friday
at about 10 PM you can catch me watching ladies

shaking they boo-ty
let me be ea-sy
and allow someone else to take control of the M-I-C

Inside The Eye of a Hurricane

Caught inside this beautiful plane
inside the eye of a hurricane
where demons and blessed angels reign
inside the eye of a hurricane
poetic maniacs, mad poets
out of order in brains
live for the words, not for the fame
some people die, others fall to shame
inside the eye of a hurricane
complete, it's a circle
with magnificent pain
not a game, that's too tame
you can win or lose those things,
this is something more
this right here is insane
inside the eye of a hurricane
it's subject to change
you'll find the pattern
is unpredictable
category serious, actually
call it memorable
this moment is golden
new age call it platinum
but that's all forgettable
like storms without eyes
making hurricanes synthetically lyrical
kind of like a miracle
one in which can't be tamed
going against a monster turned pretty

all in God's name
they can call it blasphemous
but they're limited in their aim
un-brainwash yourself
put your stake in a new claim
it's love, it's hell
inside the eye of a hurricane.

Let Me Tell You

I want to tell you now
just in case you haven't heard
I love you
you hear that
I love you.
Today is good enough to say it
and I can't risk til we're in heaven
so it's a quarter past seven
and I'm calling just to say
I love you.
While standing in the rain
after it was 96 degrees
arms wide open
waiting for the Universe to hug me
there's no need to explain it
even though I could say it backwards in my sleep
you love I,
I hope so
cause in my heart is where I keep
the memories, the little things
even when it all starts to sting
baby, through you I breathe
when I say
I love you
I love you
please believe me when I tell the world
I love you.
It means so much more when I'm here alone

when convo is only held through the phone
when internet waves seem so monotone
my friend, best believe
I love you
with all I got
even with my reserves
I love you
coming out of left field
sending you a telegram
saying that
 I love you
under moon lit skies
not waiting til you're there
I love you
lost one, girl I never told
I love you
homeboy, brother from another mother
I love you
to anyone who thinks I hate them
I love you
life is too short
way too short,
so don't forget
I love you.

Relax, Relax

Life can be reactive sometimes
causing one stress tax
bs all around
kicking anger levels to the max
but the swift peace I get from heaven
helps to keep my mind on track
Universe whispering in my ear
relax, relax.
I find I get dissed sometimes
they think the poetry is whack
it's not this, it's not that
a bit minus of the facts
my place to reign at the top
figuring, I might not get a crack
keep whispering in my head
relax, relax.
Here they come with the bum rush
they want to know, placing taps
how I keep this thing moving
computers they want to hack
but the fire inside of me
it's not meant to be trapped
underdog subconscious saying
relax, relax.
Avoiding traps, on contact
I have to counteract
fo sho', it's not a show
watch all this fade to black

got a knack to make it happen
catching you while ya nap
they can't believe it, can't perceive it
relax, relax,
because it's a different hat where I'm at
try to sit where I sat
9th inning with two outs
but guess who's up to bat
life can be reactive sometimes
I'm going to knock it straight off the map
as long as I keep the ability to stay calm
forever I am relaxed.

Rock-Solid-Words

Rock-Solid-Words
causing avalanches and earth shakes
small to large quakes
are felt from poetic cell membranes
if you start casting stones
you're throwing my verbs around
nouns knocking down
so called great writers
I'm Tighter than the End on the Offensive line
and most of your lines are offensive
poems 50% explicative
and this soap box won't help
but I'm a nutcase on full auto
old soul makes it so my blast be from the past
and I'm not too glad I have to be the lamb
some would say sacrificial
but I'll make this official
I'm eating up my own emotions
cause I'm
-Rock-Solid-
with Words stacked sky high
don't need a tower of Babel
don't plan to listen to you babble
why must I hear the ramble
if it's nonsense condensed in forms of compact ish
cleaned this up a bit for the benefit
of those who don't approve of cursing
but you might not want to read my next verse
cause sometimes I feel cursed

like someone is plotting my hurt
setting up my death
but I'm,
Rock-Solid
with Words that are breakable
when broken down
the gem can be found
and when I come to town
expect the shine
this light before it fades
this life before it phase-s
I'm amazed that
this is a process that is constantly repeated
undefeated warrior feeling constantly depleted
I wonder how do you perceive it
my achievements vs. believe-meant
this starting to sound like politics
so let's switch
back and get focused on the subject
Rock-Solid-Words
used as foundations to plantations
cornerstone of a nation
you can't get rid of this
I'm the object, objected
when lawyers call for objections
won't be no second guessin'
or second comings
unless,
you need Jesus in for that lesson
or Mohammad if you rather take that direction
it tends to get complex and

the choice is yours
we open doors to give excitement
and if you like this
then imagine what it feels like to get hit with
Rock-Solid-Words
now spit!

Soul Brother Number II

I base this poetic case
on events laid complacent
from convo between me and you,
so as I shape this
I'm up in your face with
something that can be viewed as brand new,
so don't mistake it or misplace it
cause what it's laced with
fits your lungs with fresh breath you could chew,
so when my presence graces
your existence changes, please stop complaining
my spirit's bringing the power you once knew,
so lose that self containment
only you can change that
you'll get your blessing when this you do,
because your gift has been placed
your pain erased
for it's been replaced with
soul brother number II.

This Is To You Pops (2005)

At 27
I still look forward to Sundays
to watch Nascar or football
like I did when I was 12,
only now
I have to tell you
who's on what team
because sometimes you can't remember.
I laugh,
because you still find a way to be funny
you know,
you're the first comedian I knew
and somehow
you're still rolling
sometimes due to old age
it's amazing how you do so many things
so well.
No doubt, it hasn't been easy
but I wouldn't replace
and no man can imitate
what it is you do
are doing, have done
providing guidance
spiritually, mentally
physically it's a part of why I'm a big success today
just being alive
with peace of mind

suites me fine in these days and times
so, here's the testimony to let you know
your prayers went through
for your son
thank you father
my dad
my oldman
my pops
know that
I'll always be looking forward
to another Sunday
to sit and live
by you.

Truth

Truth,
yeah truth is as truth does
but the truth is
half the world don't want to tell it
¾ don't want to hear it
and when you say it
people say they rather have a lie.
I'm like damn, I am the truth
so it's no wonder I get rejected
get disrespected
shown up and out from some
frontin' mickey fickey
shouldn't be picky
but listen
I've been standing for the truth so long
I don't know where to sit
because I got him, her, them, you
telling me five different things
five different perspectives
and everybody suppose to be right
yeah right, I keep hearing a bunch of hype
from people protecting their own interest
protecting their own ass
so should I get mad or laugh
when someone tries to gas
me, I keep thinking to myself if he
or she would just be straight with me
I could relax a little
but it's too little too late

and the last date I went on wasn't that great
since hidden agendas got put up on the teleprompt
I'm like, for real,
she didn't think I'd see this coming
skip running,
I'm jumping head strong into the situation
cause what I'm facing
is 5 to 10 lies per second
I want to believe yo ass
but if the past taught me not to be a sucker
then shame on me again if I haven't learned
I'm concerned in this modern day and age
who's not out to get paid
even if it's paid off
people sell their soul for chicken and a biscuit
then still want to be your friend
still want to shake your hand
still want to understand
why you question every motif
and I would blow this all off
but that's not going to happen
there's a small fraction of those I don't oppose
but shoot, I can't trust them either
so in order to make any kind of move
I up my faith and replace this long stance
for the truth
cause now-a-days, I can't afford it
even when it's free
don't you know that's how you get viruses
in your mainframe in the first place,
here's a taste of truth
and I hope it suits ya

if not, then oh well
you probably didn't care anyway
and the way it's looking,
people have three different plans
to cover their asses anyway
if he don't fit the bill
some other sucker will pay
and hey,
don't get mad cause I tell it how it is
I just want those who have some type of clue
to recognize truth when they see it
truth when they smell it
so when it's time to swallow
they won't choke on the smoke blown daily
cause in the end
you can't straddle the fence with a maybe
cause truth will snatch yo ass
smack you in the face
and say,
HEY, I'M THE TRUTH,
now what'cha gon' do
about that...
The Truth.

What-Is-Stress (2006)

Somebody came up and asked me
what-is-stress
and the only reply I could give him was
when-you-do-your-best
and find you still don't get no rest
because that wasn't good enough
take me for example,
I'm in my late 20's
and work as a TA in the public school system
consensus say I should get paid less to teach
but the answer is not that simple
because during school time
my name is no longer Mr. Williams
it's daddy
and even though I'm not married
I got 22 kids trying to hold my hand
asking can I walk with you to lunch
because they know when it's time to go home
no father is going to be there
it won't be playtime with daddy
throwing balls in parks
or taking the neighborhood kids

to the movies after dark
it's not enough that mommy tucks them in
and then they yell out daddy
during a nightmare
wanting to run into strong arms,
the whole time, thinking it was me they could run to
knowing there's not much I can do
feeling the repressed regressed hate
the original daddy should have chased away
but before I could address it
somebody came up and asked me
what-is-stress
and the only reply I could give her was
when you-do-your-best
and that's still not enough
like when I touch lives
from street preaching poetry to the people
that got rejected from the church
because their clothes didn't equal
standards of society
and the sins God forgave them on
still carries on in the mind of
holy rollers, religious scholars,
self proclaimed martyrs
who give away sofas
but ask for your soul back on tomorrow

won't die for a religion they claim to believe
but send their sons and daughters over seas
to cop Gs and send bullets in hearts of
so called enemies
it's real easy to kill someone
while they on they knees
and really, let me ask you a question
if six men came to your house
with automatic weapons
would you give up in the name
of someone else's freedom
and while these thoughts you concenvin'
I wasn't relieved when
two people came up and asked me
what-is-stress
and the only reply I could give them was
when you-do-your-best
and you still feel like the more was only less
made your spirit digress
as you digest misquoted facts and welfare systems
corporate companies making billions
yet I keep passing homeless hurricane victims
people debating that these people are really lazy
let me see you start from scratch
with nothing, have you looking crazy
and maybe, oh just maybe

I could be wrong
but instead of giving a helping hand
we fighting over who's bootlegging songs
gas prices unjustifiably rising
but instead of just throwing fits
the new reality show comes on at 8 o'clock
and we want to see who's throwing fists
I was with an AIDS patient the other day
and they had only one wish
I thought it would be to rest in peace
but instead they asked me this
could you please tell me
what-is-stress
and the only reply I could give was
it's when you-do-your-best
and still don't pass the test
cause I felt satisfied I spent
one hundred and sixty five
dollars to get good seats for 3 kids
to watch a basketball game
only for the star player to get ejected
and their one request was to get his autograph
but their chance got rejected
when he started talking trash
stuck up his middle finger
and got suspended from the team

and his answer was that he's chilling in his
45 million dollar dream
there was no need to model his role
even though he don't know he just confused 3 kids
and instead of me being the hero
they wondering how can they get the cream
he has, never mind how he acts
and since that's all that he could teach
when he passed
these same kids reached warped conclusions
and to me they asked
what-is-stress
and the only answer I could give them was
when you-do-your-best
and I must confess
that in this text I tried to find the solution
but the more I kept writing
all I found was air pollution
and even in my search for truth
people told me they rather have a lie
so I paused for a second
prayed to God and asked why
how-when-where and
what-is-stress
some how staying stuck on
when you-do-your-best

no matter how I spit this text
could stand in line for hours
and when they ask who's next
I raise my hand to be acknowledged
but there's no cure for being perplexed
or getting vexed
in other words, I'm getting pissed
cause they not answering my question
and I'm past second guessing
I've asked it six times in these lines
and still can't find the lesson
leaving bad impressions so I stay confessing
that what I'm looking for
must not be worth asking
because I just keep getting ignored
so on the seventh time I put it forth
my quest is going to be complete
and, it may take you a week to figure out
but that's only when you seek
to find the peace I received
after constantly asking
what-is-stress
and I can not tell now, since I let it go
think about it
and may you-be-blessed.

What's Behind a Bullet

I – hear – bul – lets
in the midst,
bullets flying, burying deep in chests
shot from guns in defense
some consider offense
but always…always
in hate.
Bullets, man-made
lead, copper, casing and black powder
meant only to bring death
not safety,
safety is peace
not from a piece shooting bullets
yes bullets
I hear bullets in the midst
whizzing, thudding, thumping
ricocheting,
bullets moving-all-around
you not understanding man
you're not sitting behind this car
with bullets flying over your head
you're not feeling hot heat
from neighboring countries, the police
or militant killers who'll kill you with
bullets,
golden bullets, silver bullets
bullets with your name on it
hollow point, highly explosive
armor piercing bullets

I hear them in the midst
bodies dumping, muscles convulsing
dreams I can't forget
bullets, bullets, bullets – BAM
they constantly getting shot
bullets, bullets, bullets – BAM
who's next to get popped
bullets over broadway
who's number one with a bullet
happy-trigger-fingers
itching just to pull it,
I hear bullets man
you think it's a game people playing
until they drive-by
until this flies by
until you wake up one night
sweating bullets
standing in the hot sun
ducking bullets, yea bullets,
bullets shot in defense
some say offense
and I – hear – bullets – in – the – midst
deadly, oh so deadly
I can feel them rip
through souls of lost children
bullets, they shooting bullets
caps, buckshots, projectiles
little missiles
I'm talking bullets,
it doesn't matter the name
the results are the same
the ending is your death

and I hear
bullets – in – the – midst
bullets – in – the – midst
flying high, being buried
deep inside chests
shot from guns in defense
some say offense
but I'm convinced
that it's always…always
in hate.

When I Realized I...
(dedicated to Ebony)

My spirit finally realized
how beautiful you are
and at first my reaction was like
oooooo, but
instead of wasting it with
the impure teaching of my peers
I embraced your spirit with the Universe
and felt what it really meant to love a sister
my sister
poetically, just like me.

You Ain't Got No Power

It was kind of funny
to hear a man beg for his life
after seeing him claim a day earlier
that he was omnipotent.

There is No Tomorrow

A Reason

I sat outside in a gravel pit
atop a park bench
after having a "blah"
type of feeling towards the world
-and-
as I was waiting for my day to turn around
a second grade class
proceed to lunch
in one of those
straight lines we grew accustomed to being in
during elementary school
-when-
a little Black girl looked over
and waved at me
because…

Displaced

It matters not the time, or even the place
when almost everything you know in an instance
gets erased
there's a bit of uncertainty that now must be faced
it's here, it's there
for now you are
displaced.

At Thirty

To be honest
I'm just grateful to be alive
didn't think I'd see past 25
cause in my eyes
I saw my own demise
the plight of this nation makes a soul brother realize
that it'd be wise not to coincide
with the drama that sometimes applies
to how we livin'
to the state we're in
your enemy could be your closest friend
your next of kin
I just don't understand
things won't go back to how they were back when
it was a sin to show too much skin
traded swords for bullets
instead of spoken words for pens
I cringe at how we spend
opinions like fortunes
sometimes you can't mend broken bridges
that broke hearts within
so again, you may not comprehend
on how I've moved from one to ten
from this to then
I tend to do that see,
grateful now to just be at thirty.

Elimination

I face elimination daily
24/7, 365 days, every year
in every category, in every place
this is directly related to my race
no place is safe for me
there is no security
even family keeps killing me
genocide, world wide describes
Black on Black crime,
I am the news reported at every hour
if not guilty,
then speculated and debated
as a man to fear
the world believes
I beat my wife, my kids
kill innocents in the names of
money, lust and power
even history proves I'll go against God
in any religion that's documented
wars that use to be dictated
are now regulated by bullets I shoot
confusion I believe and foreign eyes eyeing me
as the current modern day slave
roads are constantly paved by my hands
and my blood,
suppose-to-hide
my tears
as cheers come from profiting peers

when I'm incarcerated
my family faded
long before I believed I was a hustler
now mothers call me
baby daddy
no good nigger
and you figure I would have caught the drift by now
but I'm too interested in chasing
hoop dreams, cash schemes
to entertain the masses as the newest gladiator
they call it sports but what support
is given by multi-millionaires
to reconstruct Black leadership that was
-Eliminated-
when Martin and Malcolm was
-Assassinated-
I lay incapacitated
even though I believe I made it
by getting out of the hood
but what good does it do my own kind
by leaving others behind
in warfare I care not to explain
a setup that's far from a game
but things remain the same
actually, it's getting worse
as our children keep filling special education classes
and college courses only prepare us to pass
as a contributing member to a capitalist system
not meant to promote unity or community
it sounds better with I, myself and me
cause we keep focusing on

videos, hoes and more dough
and the elevated conscious is a no-no
look at Black Panthers, Black Churches
divided now because we can't work
together in the need to stop the death we keep facin'
I wonder now is it too late to save face and
our souls as people, it's past complicated
how much longer will it take
before we as a people are permanently
-Eliminated-

Freestyle Friday -Part X-

Let's send this one off the radar
I'm that dot on your map
label me B -major-
and I'll wager you your poetic skills
I'm a number one hit
get so live on my old school style
you can see words coming off my spit
as I slip letters into diction from
notebooks I scribe in
I've been one to watch for
but I've been kept underground
so I can Harriet Tubman similar poets
into the matrix
if these are the brakes
I'm scootin' off with all of the cake
including yo piece
see I seek that zone Miles Davis stayed in
call me Rebirth of the Cool
drool dropped from the bottom of my lip
as I go deep inside my pool
of thought
see what I brought to the picture
makes the sun that much better
and I'm drying them all up
no broken record from my poetic scriptures
so let's figure this out like simple mathematics
B-D plus O-T
sums up to one fantastic poet
screaming down your city blocks

like I just escaped a court room
yet why is it when you hear some of these lyricists
they starting to sound like I do
see we can take it back to my Miles Davis reference
and hey, all wanna-be poets
it's from me that makes the Birth of You
copyright that 2007
and trademark my pen name too
and who is gonna come to this mic
it seems there are very few
that are ready to rock
who's ready to pop
and do like poets do?

Here's To My Education (2005)

I work at a bookstore
for, seven dollars a hour.
Got my...BA degree and diploma
for what,
so I can tell society
that I'm educated enough to get a
J-O-B,
but...I work in a bookstore
for seven dollars a hour.
I'm not mad
no need to be
as I see my education
in books for
35.99,
that's before my 30% discount
a bit more was the total for my college books,
but oh well
can't beat the 30% deal,
now reading other people's opinion
seeing what it takes to get rich
in three months to three years
and who needs an education
with this info right here,
what good is my diploma now
when I'm doing what I'm doing
without Algebra II and Shakespeare
because I'm,
in this bookstore

for, seven dollars a hour
and none of my education
is stopping my feet from hurting now
oh well,
I think I'll go prove reading is fundamental
doing what my resume reads
I'm overqualified to do
and that is,
work in this bookstore
with my education.

Hunger

Hunger,
it can make you reconsider your faith
thinking twice when you see
someone real happy,
eating…
and you hungry.
Hunger,
will make you look again when you broke
at someone who's banking so much cash
and they wasting it on bullshit
while you struggling
to pay last months bill.
Hunger,
will turn that little bit of hope
that made you smile for a second
into frustration when,
so many people are succeeding
and you're bleeding from the heart
because you got turned away again
from another
six-dollar-job.
Hunger,
has you awake at night
because you can't stop thinking of
how things should be
but misery keeps ruining your parade
people say
smile, it'll be ok
but they have no idea that

hunger,
is keeping you so mad
that you can't concentrate
on the good things
making you seem mean
and get called bully
from repressed stress
let out on innocent prospects,
hunger has you considering death
in a different way
it's not hard to see
suicide, homicide
not going out alive
whether it be robbing a bank
or robbing your life
and if you think that's trife
know that
hunger can make it so I kill your wife
for the price of ice
and now
that it don't look so nice
it is hunger
making it so you realize
it's do or die
hunger
you can see it in my eyes
hunger
can make you laugh
but makes most people cry
hunger,
when that empty feeling
finds your soul,

your body isn't the only thing the knows hunger…

In That Number

Oh when the saints
go marching in
oh when the saints-go-marching in
oh I want – to be in that number
when the – saints – go – marching in…
but what the hell do you do
when the saints come running out?
What do you do
when there's no where to go
and the last word you heard was
you can't stay here no more
we've run out of money for you
sorry, but I'm just doing my job.
Family displaced like this was the slave trade
son in Texas, brother in Atlanta
husband still floating down the river
grandmother got a sheet over her body
on the express way
father right beside you
but his mind lost in space
and no,
there will be no relief
and no,
bottled water is not available,
and no,
the Bush burning is not God,
it's the president in Iraq fighting for democracy
sending troops to fight so called terrorist
sending millions of your tax dollars to destroy

then build up the same nation
but,
he won't be sending you any FEMA checks
he won't be sending you any solutions
he won't even send in the national guard
unless you're looting the stores of their resources
which includes the ones you need,
so when the first line
gets finished fulfilling their desires
you can expect the 2nd line to give you respect
but that's about it
because your life got
washed away when the levees broke
and there's no hope, no help
and the gift at the present is,
no future
causing you to stay up because you can't sleep
prescribed pills don't bring peace
so what's hurricane relief
if nightmares bring nothing but grief
mind playing back now how you couldn't hold on
after six long hours with the baby in your hand
gripping the light fixture with the other because
the water is rising
and the pressure is rising
and somebody in here is bound to die
if you let go,
and when you let go
the word no can't be screamed long enough
the word no can't be screamed loud enough
and despite people trying to hold you up
you can't stop thinking about the what if

can't stop thinking about the baby's cries
and the whys or lies don't give answers
they just give heartache and company
and even though somebody told the evacuees
they had to leave
they forgot to say sorry
we're not providing you with transportation
so, if you in the hospital
best of luck to you
you disabled,
hope God provides a miracle,
you old,
maybe you'll die before you suffer
you young,
then you'll learn from this
you Black,
you'll be waiting a few days
before someone thinks it's ok to help ya
you White,
refer back to the last three lines
because nobody is safe here in New Orleans
especially in the lower 9th ward
cause the conspiracy theory says there was a boom
so called experts say it was just a breaking sound
either way, the flood gates are open now
and I hope you can swim
because the phrase up the creek without a paddle
is an understatement
and no one is coming for you
no one is coming for you
no-one-is-coming-for-you
so in the meantime

you can sit back on your roof top in 100 degree heat
hang out in that tree and watch debris float by
you can even try to hold out in the Superdome
but ya might pass out due to overcrowding,
backed up plumbing
-and I see the saints running-
but where to cause on this bridge
you got residents in neighboring cities
not allowing access to evacuees
calling them, refugees
calling them, thugs
calling them, niggers…
TV showing chaos
like gunfights and looters
pictures projecting a thousand words
media promoting a million lies
an example is help is coming
an example is supplies are coming
an example is support is coming
but No-Body-Is-Coming-For-YOU
you want the truth
I hope you got a pound of salt
cause a grain won't erase the pain
or the memories or reality
and someone told me
that you're feeling suicidal,
and you might just be better off dead
cause if some had their way
you would be
when the levees broke
they thought you should be
and despite my intentions

I could be putting too much stress on this
but there's a question and you haven't answered it,
what the hell do you do
when the saints
come running out
and,
what do you do when there's no where to go
and you're left all alone with no one to help
it's a year later
and while it took Spike Lee to bring publicity
through a documentary
it's five years from 9/11
and they still singing God Bless America
but not for the saints
not for New Orleans
somebody keeps calling your name out
but it has more to do with Madi Gras
not about how you're handling self doubt
and, if you're a minority from this section
I wonder if you're still waiting on your
40 acres and a mule to be given to you
still waiting for your civil rights
still waiting on lady justice
for hate crimes against your kind
in your mind you may still be waiting
on a system that's using any kind of way
to keep you running
but the only thing running
are mouths
the only thing running
are the saints
the only thing running

is me out of breath
because I'm still waiting on the saints to come
marching in
cause when they do…
I pray to God that the true saints will be
in that number.

One More Time

Today just may be
the last day for me to breathe
the last one to see,
the last to…be.
One last chance to take life for what it means
the last to fulfill the opportunity
whether I dis- or agree
no more next time, only memory
it's the last call to run free
rather it be positive or full of negativity
will I be pouting or might I cheese
in the day or dark, might it shine or be cloudy
could be plain humble or go out rowdy
no more expressions
so someone else does the talking
may go from running, to not even walking
just my soul because there isn't a being
it'd be too late to drop that seed
no mouth, no brain, no soul to feed
permanently gone, no longer earthly
can take it slow or in a hurry
all at once or in multiple flurries
some might even say I went to early
say all the troubles I had are now buried
yesterday is gone and tomorrow is no worry
because today just may be.

Proving My Innocence

Well, since I'm guilty
let's skip the court cost, lawyer fees
and society eyeing me as
guilty,
yeah, you know I did it
because I'm Black
and when a White woman gets
smacked, kidnapped
or goes into relapse
somehow, I have to be the cause
somehow involved in the downfall
why be appalled
because…I'm guilty.
Forget evidence because people are convinced
I did it, I said it
regardless if it's hearsay, speculation
or my all time favorite
your personal opinion,
oh my how much that counts
and holds weight
because I'm guilty.
For a second
I thought about pleading insane
but then I'd have to maintain
being crazy,
I thought I was normal but
a psychologist deemed me schizo-
you know because I don't
except for that fact

that I'm guilty.
So there's no more need for
breaking news or shocking clues
my attitude won't be at all rude
because I'm that dude
you can always look to
for being guilty,
that's right
if it's wrong,
it's me.

She Endured Long Nights

She endured the long nights
no telephone calls
waiting for that
quick message
be it text or via pony
just as long as she knew that
he was ok
doing well, still breathing
she damn near feein'
just to be frustrated with his bullshit
at least with this
she'd know he was there
by her side, still alive
not out on a limb
where she'd have to go get him
knowing the branch can't take the weight
or the pressure,
world on her shoulders
and she still making the moves
still finding a way to smile
all the while
her life tumbling down Mount Rushmore
cause at the front door
hear come the cops a knocking
BOOM BOOM BOOM
opening up to heartbreaks, headaches
and shit she didn't ask for
see, you don't know about this

about these times where she wishes
she never stepped out on "Take a Chance Lane"
about the times
she's spent supplying the dead sea with liquid
she wants to be resurrected
but check it
God don't come on crunch time
or lunch time
since the Divine's clock set to infinite
her's locked onto eight
the Universe already sent the answer
yet she's coming up 60 minutes late
so the date is just as blind as three mice we see run
and before you know it
here comes the son
but not the man we thought it to be
it's the one leaving her lonely
saying sorry
saying nothing
cause he ain't got anything to say
can smell the quick fifth of liquor
is about all He-nne-say
or gonna say
and I may be looking too far into it
but I too cherish the day
when she no longer has to endure
but can truly be
happy, without having to be
endured.

Soul Trap

she walked through the door quietly
even though it was **H**ell outside
and the rage lay within
she could use a friend
but "it" would never allow that
won't allow that love in the room
to consume her being
because love don't live here no more
or, it no longer lives there
behind the rib cage and right next to another breath
she chases that **A**way
not knowing it's what's going to save her
if only she could see
but, blind are the eyes to negative ways
when she believes that's all she knows
a lie,
not worth telling but for some reason
believable...and
Trouble never looked so good
until it's consequences that must be paid
unlike dues
this could've been prevented
Even still, she's wrapped up in it
Killing her soul slowly
and what am **I** to do for
i'm not her dad, her uncle nor her close relative
but what's relative is

i care,
enough to Let go so Life can be
what it is
because i'm doing what i'm suppose to
but even i must admit
that in order to destroy hate
"i" had to make it So love
could take away the pain
even if it wasn't my fault for hate
being there
in here,
in the first place.

Third World Vision

When you awake
I bet the slobber on your pillow is still fresh,
and the warmth under your covers
has you wishing to stay in bed
five – more - minutes.
When we get up
we are welcomed by flies
dry heat and a smell of fresh goat shit,
there's no warm pancakes with whole milk
we about to go kill our breakfast
if we can find it.
I dreaded waking up this morning
because it's another day, not another dollar
of making it through hell.
So while you prepare for work, class
making visits to bathrooms to freshen up your face
I'm replacing the spot
where this dead kid was laying
with dirt and rocks
because I got tired of seeing
the carcass sitting outside
making me want to vomit.
It's 10 A.M. and my troubles running so deep
you could drop a penny for my thoughts
and I'd find a way to give you change.
There's a war going on outside
but instead of watching it on CNN
I smell it, hear it, taste it
right down to my teeth.

Instead of reading the newspaper
in the last hours of the morning
or sharing a muffin with a friend
I huddle young men inside a closet
telling the approaching rebels
"There's No Young Warriors Here!"
not to fight their war
there, won't be no more guerilla tactics
destroying my village
they'll have to kill me first
can you picture my thirst for what it is you have
the ability to live
because here, we only survive.
This is far beyond what you find
in your rough streets
almost everyone in those parts
are innocent bystanders
not just the girl who got shot playing double dutch
no, here we clutch our ears as we duck
bullets coming from cold blooded men
fighting over land
not worth the blood spilt on it.
I would,
rather be running for my health
not my life
studying about economics
wishing I could make money to barter for peace,
but instead, I'm witnessing
two thirty-three year old men
with a machete and a sub-machine gun in hand
hem up this thirteen year old girl
because they want some pussy.

You got,
girls gone wild
we got,
girls getting raped
daily,
forget a future or making babies
having families, being happy
growing old, getting wiser
even the energizer bunny loses power
but here, we losing our wills to live.
Missionaries keep trying to teach us about Jesus
the Holy Spirit and God
telling me He's all there is and He is omnipotent,
but, I think they're ridiculous
and his power seems impotent
because we all dying.
I can't even get along with my so called brothers
so what's this white Jesus going to bring,
is it the pain that still stings as rich white men feen'
to move us off what dirt we can claim
and, no matter how hard I keep trying
I can't pray away A.I.D.S., plagues and all this hate,
my fate is a question
your place is a blessing
but no one is helping me
better yet we, us
you all too busy dancing at parties,
out here you better run and hide
so I step, step, side to side
but not because the music is live
it's because of genocide
watching-the-explosions-all-around-me

watching-the-explosions-all-around-me
watching-the-explosions-all-around-me
lighting up the midnight sky
I think it's day
wanting to fly myself out this
no-fly-zone
because I want to be free…
give us, us free
but that's a mockery
an unfulfilled dream
that even Martin Luther King didn't see.
I got a promise land
and it's anywhere but here
anywhere far from this
Third World Country,
where representing what I am
won't leave me dead because
someone thought I wasn't worth the air I breath
please,
my vision is like your lady justice
a tease.
There's no love, no hope
and no you here
in this Third World Hell.

This Thing Called Poetry

If nobody won't do it
then it will be me, right here
pushing this thing till my brain shuts down
til God comes back through Jesus
and says let's go
I'm going to roll this scroll out and do this thing
called P-O-E-T-R-Y
because I'm a P-O-E-T
straight down to the soul,
crowds upon crowds
come to hear people spit out loud
but it's nothing if it's not created deep
beyond the mind and through out the heart
it's more than my line of work
it is me, like love
you can't separate the B from the Dot
like you can't stop this lyric
this spirit, this pen from pressing lead into paper
during the midnight hour
when I should be sleep
at work, when I should be working
in my dreams putting together words into phrases
that captivate life situations
that has people debating who's the best
or what's the worst poem they ever heard
but that's not my concern
cause my feelings been hurt before
and I've been ignored

but you can't stop this thing called poetry
and I'll be right here
sweating away as I yell out lines
to poems that don't rhyme
freestyle even if it don't make since
screaming this stanza so loud
my mouth gets dry
and I can taste the blood in my throat
I eat, drink and poop out poetry
I find other poets on the same mission
and listen in the cypher as they quote facts
sing hymns, make points and put out
information you should take in
I begin when the thought ends
and recycle what I don't use
I-Spit-That-Poetry
with or without mics
calm but they like it when I'm hype
in Raleigh, Durham, G-Boro
on the internet, in the car, with my dog
to a kid, up in the air
I don't care where it takes place
cause this is what poets do
and I can only explain in bits and pieces
try to fit it in a thesis how we make sense common
and abstract, relax jack cause I got this one here
I even got my own theme music
in a beat box starting way before hip hop
under the sun in Africa
to drums made of goat skin and wood
update it and they may say I got rhythm
back date it and it would be blues

integrate it and it's R&B
and there you'll find me with similar artists
kicking knowledge with feet coming out our mouths
this is my verbal kickball
and I be the homerun hitter,
the clutch guy, the equalizer
call me off the bench and I'll be the 6th man
be chanting de-fence, de-fence
it's so necessary
see I, heard last week on an APB
that I'm the most wanted revolutionary
and I carry my cause in-between these two ears
in my thoughts
but since I don't want to be known as a lot of talk
I keep writing poems on anything available
so when my books come out
you may find that I scribed
on napkins, the back of a program
get so desperate I have to use the palm of my hand
cause I can't keep these two lines in my head
long enough to put them down
30 minutes from now
so the mere fact that I'm spitting this here poem
amazes me
because daily I probably forget
5,000 words worth of diction
and that's because sometimes I don't pay attention
listen, there's about to be a word jacking
taking place, so get your hands up
I got this mechanical pencil full of lead in yo face
and I dare you to try to write a poem with me
because that's only gonna get me hype

and I could keep this up all night
but since that ain't right and I'd rather write
you now can now have back your open mic.

To You, The Victim (Revised)

As I step my way to the forefront
I pass last minute attempts and distractions
of cheesy store sales and nonessential magazines,
people busy
going about a normal routine
like this lady holding her baby
and that store clerk sweeping the floor…
they've got no clue on my intentions
no warning to you, the victim that,
THIS IS A MOTHER FUCKING STICK UP
AND YOU GOT TWO MINUTES TO GIVE ME
ALL YOUR FUCKING CASH
SO DON'T FUCK WITH ME
BECAUSE MY BULLETS GOT NO NAME
NOW, RUN YO SHIT
and as my demands are made to the cashier
the pure fear in the room has escalated so high
I got a man pissing in his pants
and a woman clutching her chest
searching for breath,
for many, time has stopped
and the only thing that matters
is making it to the next moment
hoping they will get to see tomorrow
or their spouse
a friend,
maybe even the dog
but to me

none of that shit matters
because all I'm counting on
is this next minute and thirty-six seconds
to elevate myself of this pressure
of weekly checks and bullshit healthcare
nobody aware to the fact
that my life has been trashed,
but I've remedied that now as I yell,
MOTHERFUCKER DO YOU WANT TO DIE
STOP MOVING SO SLOW
I KNOW THERE'S MORE CASH THAN THIS
so I now demand that
EVERYONE COME OFF
THEIR JEWLERY AND WATCHES
even though I've had four years of college
knowledge doesn't feed me at night
it doesn't help me when I'm looked over
for some unqualified person who
only had a connection
never mind my experience
or my dedication to my responsibilities
how I was humbly taking life's shit
moving on about my day
how I looked to be needed
but everyone was too busy to talk
or hear my concerns,
and as I think of this
I notice I'm down to a minute and four seconds
with what appears to be a hero in the making
by the soda isle
so I go
SAY THERE STUPID FUCK

YOU MUST WANT
TO MEET DESTINY TODAY
BECAUSE YOUR BRAVERY
IS GONNA LEAVE YOU BURRIED
SO I ADVISE YOU TO NOT ACT
LIKE THE BAD ASS YOU DREAMING TO BE
YOU BETTER GET ON YOUR KNEES
AND PUT YOUR HANDS WHERE I CAN SEE
OR YOU CAN CATCH THIS
BLA-BL-OOOWW,
shooting a bullet into the air
makes everyone realize I'm truly serious,
that the only distance between me and them
is the ¾ inch of trigger space and a firing pin
connecting with a casing full of gun powder
with a hollow tip at the end,
damn it, I've wasted enough time
only forty-two seconds left
and I've barely collected enough to get me to the
next stick-up
thinking to myself this bullshit sucks
hearing a child ask
-why is he doing this-
but her young mind can't comprehend
that my faith has been depleted
future everything but defeated
as I wonder where God was
when I prayed steadily for years
the world still passing me by
there was no peace
-why-
but it's too late for that

yet, how can I turn back
cause I'm down to twenty-three seconds
and this is my chance, so I begin with
I APOLOGIZE FOR THIS
BUT I HAVE TO DO SOMETHING
AND THIS NICKEL AND DIME SHIT
ISN'T HELPING MY CAUSE
YET I SEE PEOPLE MAKING MILLIONS FROM
DOING NOTHING
MOST OF THESE POLOTICIANS
CHEATING US ALL
THE POOR GET POORER,
THE RIGHTEOUS GET IGNORED
AND WE DON'T COLLECTIVELY
COME TOGETHER AS ONE,
at this point I lower my gun
knowing this is wrong
this isn't the answer,
even though many before me
has done this for a lesser reason
mine, isn't good at all,
so in my last ten seconds
I walk out of the store
seeing my conscious
is really the subject of
you…the victim.

Trapped Inside My SELF

Behind bars that are mental
on the outside with freedom
sometimes thinking
places we should switch
to keep sinful thoughts
just what they are
to make my options
that much less
stress will rest its ugly head
on the pillow I lay
waking up every day wondering
when can my thoughts be free
people figuring I'm crazy
like liquor and beer makes one lazy
but it's not that, that I sip
it's the lust of power, money and greed
catch me every morning
opening my eyes to the everlasting
I can't escape this, I can't make bail
freedom only comes
in death,
can you see?

What American Dream

Memorial Day
should include the news of past Huey's
X's and Garvey's,
but instead of history
our memories come on stones labeled
R-I-P,
but how can he or she rest in peace
when the person in pieces
is eleven?
At eleven, ten, six and the five
o'clock hour, mankind is shown world wide
portions of gang related activity
drug infested negativity
that Black society keeps getting the blame for.
I am,
in a land where
making a dollar is bigger then
the dream America has for
a small Black child in the projects
I believe my future projects
will be to reject the infectious dream
they keep feeding our kids
and restore it with a breath called
L-I-F-E
so tell me,
where should I begin to tell a tale
of rated R times X proportions
where the kids rule over the elders
and the adults keep switching between whatever

in one of the racist nations that's still in existence,
the plots and middle passage have been set
you live the drama and climax,
this is beyond tragedy
it's a continuous nightmare in
America, North America, United States of America
where glamour and glitz
are equated to less clothes and more tits
and, isn't that suppose to be
my young Black queen on the screen
I mean, who let respect slip from their grip
with people saying
those ladies made their own decision
but division is in the false unity we think exist
because crime, pornography and injustice
aren't signs of advancing
a proclamation is only as good
as the people who respect it
so let freedom ring like school bells
where IEPs and SATs determine our ability,
they say education is our new foundation
but what good is homework if children don't do it
what good are parents
if they don't support the little ones
and what good is a teacher
if they are only motivated by money?
People fearing school boards, tax cuts
and mad black youths
here's the truth, time to swallow it
it goes down easier with Hennessey
for mothers and fathers too confused
mentally abused

and a never gonna get healed psyche
to think some folk still feel sorrow
because it was slave trade that help build Nike
but imagine the blood in this land
on Sam's hands,
we aren't even humble enough to accept a defeat
and unify in an effort to start a war to get peace
but the missing piece
is controlled by a government we rely on,
so the song I sing isn't a national anthem
it's one like Sade
as I am now the official king of sorrow
forget tomorrow
because we haven't learned from the past
so I add to the gun blast with a weapon stash,
here it go Blaa-bl-ooww, Blaa-bl-oooww
as I kill another man
the police
the guy who stepped on my shoes
the woman disrespecting
and the kid not learning the lesson,
EVERYBODY GETS-A PIECE-OF THIS,
because anger was already hate
and what it makes is
what the media shows on Cops,
in the LA Times and hourly on CNN
so that those who have no clue
can see the worst part our behavior
quickly being judged, critiqued on a scale
that balances Hollywood with my neighborhood,
and you think I'm concerned with
who will win American Idol?

Know that,
I don't care for more technology
I'm searching for harmony on another line
other than the horizon,
kids say if I'm lying I'm dying
and if you add my ancestors to me
then I've been dead one billion times over
as I detoxify myself from madness taught by dreams
made in America
and get fresher with a better day, better way
with my sister, my brother
the single parent mother
or father
all considered to be a number
in a system that's like jail,
it's the devil that tricks you to come to hell
so why do they think I'm crazy
for moving towards heaven?
But, that's ok
I choose to run because I don't need to fight today
if it means I don't have to fight one more time
against you
against them
against myself,
as I deport what's left of me
from this American Dream.

What Are Your Saying

Words are meaningless
to a dead man
and it's unfortunate I find myself
surround by fellows
who are better dead
after hearing what it is
they had to say.

When She Realized
(dedicated to Caitlyn)

One of the most beautiful things
I have ever experienced
is the moment she realized
I loved her back.

Whoever You Are, I Accept

Chemical imbalances
hidden in secrets inside cells
manifested in rapid thoughts that
seemingly don't stop
no matter the solution or seclusion.
Time doesn't heal
forgiveness does
make no mistake
the Universe holds answers
that can only be accessed spiritually,
as religion boxes it up as "God"
but let's be clear
if you can't hear what birds sing
than prayers are mere words
thrown towards heaven or hell,
may as well embrace disorder
stuck between polar opposites
drowning somewhere between
in shallow water
thinking no one understands
including yourself,
so here's the blunt truth
I accept you for what you were created to be
no matter the path taken
and the lessons learned thereof
love is the most tenacious tool
one can hold in their possession
so just know
you have been forever loved since eternity
by me.

About The Author

Billy Williams, Jr. was born to write poetry. Poetically knows as B-Dot and OnePoeticGamer, the life as a poet all started because of a girl back in 7th grade. Seeing he had a gift with words, he began to use his energy to produce poetry that spoke to various genres.

Hailing from Raleigh, North Carolina, Billy is a poet, educator, coach, gamer, streamer and motivator. Poetic Superhero is Billy's first book of published poetry, with more poetry books to be released in the near future.

If you want to find out more information about Billy's upcoming books, you can contact him by way of e-mail at onepoeticgamer@amazulugaming.com or sending a message to him from the following website www.amazulugaming.com. If you wish to know more about his gaming/streaming life, check him at www.twitch.tv/onepoeticgamer.

Social Media Contacts

Poetry Blog: www.amazulugaming.com
Instagram: Onepoeticgamer
Twitch: www.twitch.tv/onepoeticgamer

AmaZulu Gaming, LLC

Poetry Books Written By One Poetic

Poetic Superhero

Everybody is looking for a hero. Poetic Superhero is here for you.

The I prElude I (ebook only)

In order to find we, HE must find himself before finding SHE.

His Emotions Released

This is written for Her…I'm glad I finally got Her attention.

School Dad

Poetry inspired by 16 years of working as an educator in elementary, middle and high school.

the Book of HER (coming summer 2021)

Thirty-three poems written in twenty one days for the artist also known as Gabriella Wilson

Poetic Flows - A Book of Rhymes (upcoming 2021)

When I feel the flow, I let go with words.

www.ingramcontent.com/pod-product-compliance
Lightning Source LLC
Chambersburg PA
CBHW031202090426
42736CB00009B/754